The Plague Ditties

By the same author

—Novels—
The Gourmet (aka The Damned Don't Die)
Ulysses' Dog (aka The Spider's Cage)
Lethal Injection
Death Puppet
The Price of the Ticket
Prelude to a Scream
The Syracuse Codex
Dark Companion
The Octopus On My Head
Windward Passage
A Moment of Doubt
Old & Cold
Snitch World

—Poetry—
Poems for a Lady
Gnachos for Bishop Berkeley
Morpho (w/ Alastair Johnston)
Small Apt (w/ photos by Shelly Vogel)
Across The Tasman Sea
Sonnets

—Nonfiction—
Laminating the Conic Frustum

—Recordings—
The Visitor

The Plague Ditties

Jim Nisbet

Molotov Editions

San Francisco, California

Molotov Editions

5758 Geary Blvd. #221
San Francisco, CA 94121
www.molotoveditions.com

The poems collected here were written by Jim Nisbet and distributed to his email list during the Covid-19 pandemic April 30, 2020 through June 21, 2022.

A note about the text: Poems are numbered as they appeared in the emails Jim sent to his Plague Ditty mailing list. Some gaps in numerical order appear, indicated with *, but no poems are missing or omitted. Dates poems were sent are included where available.

A Slight Adios for Tom Raworth read at the Tom Raworth Memorial Tribute: April 6, 2018, presented by The Poetry Center and the Department of English at UC Berkeley

Jim Nisbet (1947-2022)

Copyright © 2023 by Carol Collier (Literary estate of Jim Nisbet)
LCCN : 2023941474

Book design by Carol Collier

All rights reserved. No part of this book may be reproduced or transmitted in any form or by any means, electronic or mechanical, including photocopying, recording, or by any information storage and retrieval system without the written permission of the author, except in the case of brief quotations in critical articles and reviews.

Printed in the United States of America.

First Edition

Cover illustration: Dance of Death: Death the Strangler, 1850.
Alfred Rethel (German, 1816–1859). Woodcut; The Cleveland Museum of Art, Gift of Robert Hays Gries 1939.620
Creative Commons Zero (CC0) designation

ISBN: 978-1-948596-01-5

My thanks to the legion of fans this excursion has accrued.
And to the editors of *Stop The World, Snapshots from a Pandemic*,
who kindly reproduced "Plague Ditty No. 2."

Preface

We

San Francisco
We came, we saw, we fucked it up
California
We came, we saw, we fucked it up
Planet Earth
We came, we saw, we fucked it up

A Slight Adios
for Tom Raworth

join us at the fire, Tom, for a
final warming of the hands

o'er the momento mori
of gentle oxidation

done blowed the frame
like everybody do

done traded the martini
for mere eternity

so much wood
so much attitude

silent satellite arcs overhead
seventeen thousand miles per hour

seems kind of slow
by the dim light of mortality

twang diminuendoed to hiss
of background radiation and tinnitus

rhyme delayed
till the singularity evaporates

predicate suspended
by time's geography

and it's eight bells, mate
duty's done, done or not

now seek repose among the spines
in the library of compelling passages

fair winds, old friend
and following seas

On The Recent Election

Often, Dexter Brown, Jr. and I
Run into Floy and her person,
Ramón, in our local park.

Thursday afternoon, for example.
Nov. 10, 2016. "I've not seen
San Francisco this quiet,"

I observed, "since the earthquake."
Indeed, the park in which we stood
Was created by the '89 terremoto,

More or less. "You know Jim," Ramón
Replied, "24,000 San Franciscans
Voted for Donald Trump."

"Ten percent of the vote?"
"Just about."
"That many...."

Ramón's eyes swiveled right,
Left. As did mine. People with dogs,
People with babies, people with people...

"They walk among us," Ramón said.

The Plague Ditties

This Be The Virus

It fucks you up, corona does
    As deep and dark as coral fuzz
(Please ignore the orifice, beneath the hair,
    That bellows within its *cordon sanitaire*.)

As alleles leech along the chain
    So fever wracks the brain
Now in Seattle, now in Brattle
    -boro: wash your peaches, avoid the beaches!

Though snug in lipid it wants a host
    To conjoin its acid misery's song
'Slimy liquid, poison' — no need to boast —
    On the beat now, hominid: cough along!

w/apologies to Mr. Philip Larkin

Behold the Take-out Menu

News hath no harridan
    Like Brent Crude Presents
Not even serological probity
    Can score a dent

Upon its carapace of perfidy
    Nor dis-embitter its blonde
Cocktail of bile, a caravansary of ignorance
    Tuned to an oligarch's smile.

A gluteus osculated as regular
    As a walking beam pumps,
No demeanor too sedulous
    Only muck to cloy the sump

Of conscience, neutrino smiles,
    A mien devoid of meaning
A Moloch never brought to Barr

While all the world is teeming
    With millepaedal Corporations
And their vile suppurations

High time to spear their writhing convolutions
    Upon the pitted tines of pitiless Revolution
Else it's back to sleep with you, hapless Proletariat,
    Strangled to dreamless Purgatory

By Kapital's coarse lariat.

No. 3

5/24/2020

Somewhere is revealed
    That the original Potter's Field
Was purchased with thirty pieces of silver
    First empursed by Judas Iscariot

Which brings up a sempiternal subcutaneity,
    A chicken-and-egg problem: did Jesus
Hip the hapless brother to his status
    As a cog in pseudohistory

Or did Judas just need the geetus?

Either way, were a prettier dichotomy
    To let down its hair and greet us
On the are-we-there-yet road to Emmaus
    We'd best rent a chariot

And try to marry it.

But hey, back to democracy in chains
    And pediatric chilblains —
Yo, Shit-for-Brains, armed and maskless
    Unvetted and vaccinationless,

Disproportionately consanguineous,
    Homeostatically unsteady,
And of considerable girth,
    Do you really think you're ready

To inherit the earth?

No. 4

Cruise Ship Bookings Jump 600%
                      GlobalNews.ca

Animatronic yellow marmots cavort
    The bulkhead projection, between
Thunderheads and speckled granite,
    As S/V *Melamine Terpsichore*,

The Captain's pinnace, makes a casual
    Three knots over the Sea of History.
"Once were whales," laves the voiceover,
    "plus that stuff on the screen, not to mention

Germs and bees and poppies with pap
    [*cf. The Saprophytic Cruisers' Rubbernecking
Companion*, pp. 77, *et seq.*] Yon undulant cnidoblastic
    Tendrils beneath the septic brine

Once were bannerols
    Of forgotten petro-states,
And now that Sun burns all the time
    There's no albedo to debate.

The Anthropocene, they called it then
    The shortest epoch ever
Whose eponyms wielded shears
    End to end, every throat

They sought to sever
    No cut did they forfend
No stupidity too clever
    Till the curve of brilliance they did bend

Till thought and work and edifice
    Blundered to their ends
Till the very species walked
    No longer, wrought

To fruitless flinders of
   Squandered truth, bits of this
Not even bytes of that,
   Spavined by inchoate creeds.

Everywhere now is sedulous torpor
   No nutrition to gorge the gap
Between stone and sky
   No thermocline to glide

All's reduced to a viscid slime
   Of amber cellulose
Veined by swart quartiles of
   Asphalt indissoluble.

Finally, amidst a planetary
   Tempest of virions begat
Of biomendacity, the hapless hominids
   Wormholed the whole shebang

To vacuous oblivion: a diffeomorphism
   Of pseudodata, valence-free,
The final dissolution of computational anatomy
   Informed by infodemic quotidia,

I.e., kablooey,
   The homeostasis hammered in,
As the weather, yo,
   Went full-time grim.

Noiseless, implacable
   Antimagnetic, intractable
Not even a peep of meaning
   No gravity, no mass

And, speaking as a mere
   Trans-sentient plasma
And pool-side docent,
   Quite the relief altogether.

When the signals stopped,
   Everybody on Mars
Thoughtfully applauded
   And kicked Dilaudid. Green

Styrofoam peanuts and orange maquillage
   Clogged the seaways for centuries
But now, as you can see,
   All is calm, lifeless, squirm-free

But — was that a bird? Unheard
   Of. A blown voxel, more likely.
No matter. We're low on mix,
   The dosimeter's on the fritz

And, referring-by-way-of-an-explanatory-
   Expostulation-to-a-synecdoche-of-the-
Former-tenant, man,
   It's hot as hell.

Time to transmogrify aloft
   Back to the mothership
Hovering beyond the belt
   Of plasticules and clockwork sludge

Got to stay on schedule
   Settle onto the hermetic afterdeck
Of *Corona Princess*, stress- and
   UV-free, with a cocktail and a scone

For we've many a dead world to visit
   Before we're safely home.

No. 5

Force majeure

…Judas Iscariot,
   Indeed,
Rhymes with lariat

As in, blow up the ballroom
   At the Marriott

Anthropo-sepsis —
   pigeons, crows, OTC anesthetics

Gawbage common currency
   What we do best, can't arrest

Plastic in emergency
   Plastic when things are normal, plastic
      The bitter end of global continuity

Lean on me, the fuck you say
   Rhymes altogether with democracy
Hacer Albóndigas De Mierda Una Vez Más
   3D print that yellow vest

Whose mother cooked this meth?
   I think it might be the best
(Besides, the fuck is progress
   Astride nuclear dystrophy?)

A singular engine splits the air
   Mid Kapital's minatory despair

A pow between the ears
   courtesy of some clown
That owns your tears

No need to don the gun muffs
   In your all-weather

Small-bore bring-a-sweater
   Panopticon

Wherein, not to worry,
   You can only, ever, hear

Everything.

*No. 7

Encircled by Browntongues:
   Sir, Sir, before you get too histrionic
May we recommend a high colonic?

Hydroxywhatchamacallit and molten casino chips
   Guaranteed to restore the smile ironic
To those nether lips, chafed and roseate

So peculiar to the morbidly blond
   (cf. *The Annals of Browntonguery*, Section Eight)

After which we can resume to hose the Proletariat
   Strip them of healthcare and retirement
Feed them space travel, rape the environment

Bait the races, saw through the traces
   Till the wheels come off
Until everybody but you,

Sir,

Has a cough.

*No. 10   6/13/2020

    Pause the pollices
        Forestall the red meat
    This breeze fresher
        Than the Speaker's gaiters:

    Injecting bleach makes you a patriot!
        Just like take-out chop suey
    Transmogrifies proles into traitors!
        Good news for Baby Huey!

    Ever indulge, Sir, the locution
        That self-immolation
    Could be your greatest contribution
        To a troubled nation?

    O Sir, Maximum Señor de Cartoonuity
        O Sir, Grief Multiplier in Chief
    Your invert gestalt ingenuously beseeches
        That you go live at five before a guaranteed

    Six or eight billion consumers of ONANVision
        The world's gratuitous organ of choice
    Roll up that sleeve, Sir,
        Apply the point

    And get the rest of us
        The fuck
            Out of this joint.

And thus, so-called American™
  So-called Democracy™
Somnambulated backwards
  Into the Bug-Zapper™ of History™.

The Paper Trail ended
  In 2001
Although, anecdotally, what followed
  Was nothing but fun.

We've got a dead planet
  And a few good leads
And we're hoping to sprout
  Civilization from seeds.

But a pall does surmount
  The mandate of our prospect
And that's how to account
  For the sedimentary layer

Of bones,
  Bones,
    Bones.

No. 12

All aboard
   The Peckerwood Express,
Somebody done strewed
   A box of crackers

Across Lafayette Square
   And little D
democracy
   Calls on the populace

Shorn of power,
   Burdened with taxes,
Recently apprised of
   'Whaaat: Slavery?'

To clean up Hizonner's mess.

Bespectacled apparatchiks
   With testicles of pepper
Wield shields translucent
   Except for their logo

Of protest-proof polycarbonate
   And batons of lead-veined wood
To beat back the avalanche
   Against a

Highstepper of dubious probity
   From beneath whose bleached polyester rug
Spew trans-delirious encomia
   Of sacral mendacity

All, all, in defiance of
   "All men are brothers;
That's the bottom line.
   If we can't take it from there

We can't take it at all."

      With all due respect to Mr. James Baldwin

No. 13   6/26/2020

"As E.U. Opens
   It Aims to Keep
Americans Out

[In] Repudiation of CENSORED's
   Pandemic [of] Blunders"
[*Emphasis added for clarity*, Ed.]
   NYT, Page 1-A and above the fold, 6/24/20.

"Not a word of it is true,"
   Bellows Baby Huey
Above the fatidic fanjets of
   Hair Farce Juan

Whose primary straphanger
   Is routinely derided
Behind his back of course
   By his Marine escort,

Many cabinet members, consultants,
   Lobbyists, sycophants, counter-jumpers,
His own wife and, I don't know, Spinoza? as
   Hair Farce Juanaldo,_P_resident _O_f_T_he _U_nited _S_windle, *aka*

El Pendejo Más Sinuoso.

This playful deployment of staff ycleptions
   Has been confirmed by 117 sources
Within and immediately clinging
   To the mucilaginous limaçon

On condition of anonymity
   Due to a Rockwell C80 fear of ostracization,
Imprisonment and death.
   —But, this just in: North Korea

Dismisses White House Lawn Logorrhea
   As <<*a promenade of wattle waddles*>>

And this: << *While pandemic waxes*
   Juanaldo wanes >> And this:

<< *Polls deal steel-toed blow*
   To Executive goolies >>
Which news, even now, is being humped
   Over the Himalayas by cheerful coolies.

But enough *ad hominem* bedevilment
   Of our dotardinal Dominium: Me, me,
Squeals la ONANVisionette, call on meee — oh
   Thank you, Sir, and all I have to say, Sir, is,

May the rotor wash never blow your perfect rug into the
   undrained colonial moat but
     If such unhappiness comes to pass, Sir, by the
Canonized Hobbes may such rug float!
   Eek,
     Sir,

You're most welcome.
   Sir! I too have question! Sir!
The hapless continuum
   Begs to know

By what own-goal further messes
   Might Global Stresses
Be exacerbated by an exponent of two
   Or four!

Because, Sir, by the office you swore,
The whole world is counting

On you!
   Yes.
     You.

Advice to Baby Huey's
    Swoonees and swoonettes,

If you want America to be first,
    Last, or anything at all,

Stop kissing his ass
    And start kissing his lips.

Full tongue.

No. 15 6/30/20

Okay. How can I explain this...

I've heard it said, in publishing, that for every equation
you put in a book,
you lose 10,000 readers.

If true, it explains a lot.

But hey! Who's publishing?

Meanwhile, like it or not, the whole world is into exponential growth.

Consider the equation

$x(t) = a \times b^{(t/T)}$

wherein

t = time

$x(t)$ is the value of x at time t

$x(0)$ = x at time zero = a

b = a growth factor i.e., how much x grows in a given unit of time, herein represented by the Greek letter T, pronounced tau. Let's declare that x doubles in three days, i.e., b = 2, and T = 3.

Now. Let's suppose that 150 people get hammered in a bar tonight, and that tomorrow morning two of them, just two, wake up with Covid 19. (A way minimal scenario.) Throw in that they are asymptomatic for three days, during which period each of them infects another two, and only two, additional people. (A way, way minimal scenario.) I.e., in three days two additional infected people yield four more infected people.

So. Leave us calculate.

At time zero, the morning after, $x(0) = a$ = the number of infected people = 2

So now we have

$x(t) = 2 \times 2^{(t/3)}$

or, number of infected people at time t equals the right-hand side of the expression, the exponent [t/3] being some elapsed time, t, divided by the time T it takes b to happen.

Let's see: The time between Memorial Day and the Fourth of July, measured in days, is 40 days.

$x(40) = 2 \times 2^{(40/3)}$

$x(40) = 20{,}643$ infected people.

20,643

People.

Get it?

No. 16   7/7/2020

Tweaker racked out
   On a bench
At the bus stop
   As flat as 95 pounds

Of wasted bones can lie
   Always the hoodie
Pulled down over the eyes
   Always the ulcerated palm

Cupped to the tinnitic ear
   On standby
Awaiting instructions
   That might never arrive.

Today, despite a sea breeze
   Grooming the willows
And nobody in sight
   A new accoutrement

A lunule of blue paper
   Obscures the mouth and nose
Its narrow metal band
   Molded to the bridge just so.

It's morning
   In America
And even the tweaker
   Is wearing a mask.

No. 17   7/14/2020

My epiglottis won't
   Let me sleep
The rest of me
   Is shot as well

The looming precipice
   Is lofting steep:
Does not the trail
   Beyond this peak

Slope straight to Hell?

And yes I have dreamt again
   The flailing dream, the one about
Failing to make the scene
   But for a forgotten mask.

Why do you ask?

Only Baby Huey is exempt
   From the global nightmare
'Cause he's living the dream, baby,
   He's got a trapdoor button and racist toadies,

Roadies packing bulletproof hairspray
   And Spawn Innanity on his TV
And Daily McInnanity
   Dealing fay twee…

And the rest of us?
   We're locked in
With the Virion-In-Chief, baby,
   Frozen in Scream.

The old dog dozes
   In the ghostly embrace

Of leathern traces of yore.
    His dream-team hitched

To the burdened sledge,
    He's racked out on the carpet
Head under the bed
    He quivers and whimpers

As the Master of None
    Mushes the phantasmagory
Balls-out to the cliff
    And over the edge

Forever to plummet
    Into the bottomless crevice
Of Yesterday's History
    Thus the ancient companion

Of humanity's misadventures
    Subsides into a proper slumber
While spindrift whirls and settles
    To fill the parallel runnels

Marking our careen.
    Now it drifts flush, then higher
Till all is effaced
    And featureless

Smooth as any tush
    In late John Updike
And an exhausted Earth
    Can sleep in silence

At last.

No. 18

Like a desert pilgrim
   Parched and scorched
Can't recall whose idea
   The stupid fast was

But can't disrecommend it
   Fast enough, no, better to have cast
The chi chi sticks with
   Some giant pig or gilded Ba'al

And got it over with,
   Win or lose,
Face down in some
   Mall massage parlor.

But now, lost and long past
   The last oasis
With its arrowed sign:
   This way to losing weight

While downing hot draughts
   Of harliquinal brine
One-on-one with the devil
   While some tame hirsute farrier

Rasps both y'alls hooves
   — What's not to like?

Please consign that semiosis
   To the Neon Museum
And send the bill
   To my delirium.

Like a comet,
   Merely to endeavor

To keep your tail
   Away from the sun?

Let only lips twitch
   In the heat, like
The ribcage of a skink
   Frozen by the glare

Of some coagulopathic sidewinder,
   While for to calculate the skitter
To the next pathetic rock, in whose shade to pause
   Meager and stalked? Better

To resort to pen and paper
   the first commandment
Of any pandemic,
   Sharpen quills by hand

As the final
   Grains of Chronos
Spiral past your duct-taped balistraria
   Like virions on the wind.

No. 19   *7/25/2020*

Safe at home in 1958
    We had Doctor Zorba
Who, his eyes turned away at last
    From the jitterbugging babe

In *The Asphalt Jungle*, weekly chalked
    Onto a dusty slate
"Man. Woman. Birth.
    Death. Infinity."

Today, not safe anywhere,
    We have Subdoctor Schnorba
Sketching in thin air
    "Person. Woman. Man.

Camera. TV." Repeat *ad
    nauseum*. Never mind
The incredulity. Expect
    Rezids, directly deposited.

Some future Pseutonius
    Will record that, despite being
Drawn by six heffalumps

Subverted to the purpose,
    Subdoctor Schnorba
Took a mid-race tumble
    From his chariot,

Despite which: We
    Have a Winner!
Reverberated off the foetid marble
    Of the viscid vomitorium.

Pseutonius, centuries
    Hence, perhaps presuming

His audience no
   Longer so dense,

Will note that the names of the
   (prominent) (white) (men)
On the race committee
   Are lost to History

As are those of the six heffalumps

As are those of the era's
   Hapless citizens

No. 20 — 8/2/2020

QED Goddammit
   Is a town in Texas
Where everybody can sit a cayuse
   And no man dwindles feckless.

Months and months
   You don't wear a mask
Then, well, you do wear one
   Ten days, more or less

—Except to church, of course,
   Where we don't allow no fabric
To come between praiseful lips
   And the Most Elevated Tympanic Membrane —

Hork-spittaw!

And now (cough) look at ya'll — sunk in sin!
   Pass the (cough) aspi(cough)rin
And let's go for a beer, hoss,
   For to wash 'em down

Maybe three or four while we're at it
   Get a good heat on, maybe toss
Up them pickled eggs & pigfeet, particolored,
   Into the jimsonweed and cow chips out back

Make room for more, har de (cough)
   Har, so as to laugh, we,
Straight up at the lid
   For all eternity.

No. 22 9/23/2020

    You just want to get shitfaced
        Tired of straitlaced
    Embrace the eco-bomb
        And declare that *they* won

    Take it away!
        This parched endocarp
    This slack-stringed autoharp
        This drowning vestibule of Zealandia

    Pull the ripcord Wreck the old Ford
        Radio wide open 107 all it would do

    Once were bloodhounds
        Tracking through tree frogs
    That one guy for whom
        The chain gang wouldn't do

    May you breathe through that reed
        In the creek under the White Oak Bridge
    Forever, brother, while the essential chicken trucks
        Thunder overhead, and maybe POTUS strokes out in bed

    O'er-stressed keeping huddled masses in line, and that corona
        Rhinderpest peculiar to odd-toed non-ungulates
    At bay, while he lies his way
        Through that tough Sunday interview

    Nobody believes a word
        But they vote for him anyway
    Cause it's all about keep-away
        Far be it from me to call it

    Caucasianization
        But from this distance, pull focus,
    It don't even look close
        To any kind of forever constellation.

No. 25 10/3/2020

Ventilator Blues

Well, you feel so disenfranchised
   We can hear you moan
Yeah, you kep' on rolling them dice, baby,
   Now listen to you moan

You got the ventilator blues, baby
   Machine's waitin' just down the hall
They start it every sunset, baby
   Just to see you crawl

Them ventilator blues, baby,
   Enough to make Small Ball bawl.

Yeah the ventilator blues, honey
   Sure to leave their mark
Yeah, the wall of TeeVees dim, baby,
   When they throw her some spark

Ain't no executive proclamation
   Got that kinda bark.
Oh, the ventilator waits
   'Case that hydroxy fails

Yeah, the ventilator waits, baby,
   'Case Big Pharma flails — or,
Asmodeus forbid, the shit's in the mail —
   Oh, that machine's been lurking, precious,

Since them Senators grew tails.

Oh! the ventilator's been waitin'
   Ever since Tulsa failed
Yeah, the machine's been warming up
   Ever since *Corona Princess* sailed

The rent's coming due, baby,
   That's Mother Nature waitin' on the couch,
Two and two been makin' five, baby,
   Long as you been openin' your mouth

Yeah, two and to been makin' five, honey,
   Ever since you lost the South
Now the ventilator's lubing up, honey,
   Keen on the bell for this bout!

But wait: you need to get the heebie-jeebies, baby,
   Just like 209,847 who came before
Yeah, here come the heebie-jeebies baby,
   Like they came for 210,346 before

Now hold on to that stainless steel table, baby,
   While the Propofol drips in
Don't think twice it's all right, baby,
   Just count backwards from ten

'Cause you got the ventilator blues, baby
   The inside of your head smells like dill
Yeah, you got the ventilator blues for real, baby
   While everybody else got ballots to fill

And if and when you wake up, maybe
   You won't have no job no more
Yeah, and if and when you wake up, maybe
   You just might be unemployed

Just like 21 million other *hoi polloi*,
   Most of whom didn't vote for you.
That's okay, boy, just mail 'em
   A pair of dice with your brand

Yeah, facsimiles of the very pair
   That are fallin' from your numb hand
Cause you got the ventilator blues, baby,

And no more time to gamble
With this troubled laaaaand…

No. 26

10/21/23

The mastodon in the bungalow
   Is CO_2 in the herebelow
And if mankind stays stepped on its penis
   This planet's gonna wind up like Venus

Where, if there's any life at all
   It's 80 miles up
In some cloud lenticular
   And altogether subsentient molecular

No county fairs
   No juicy pears
No polar bears
   No frisky mares

The dog's on the rug
   Head on the hearth
Bone on the stone
   One eye open

Cause he's wondering,
   Are these bastards
Gonna leave me all alone
   In this intemperate zone?

Bear with me
I'm just a dog:

My hyperacusis
   Getting a boost is
From all the *bulería* abroad

Authentically non-irenic
   Reliably schizophrenic
As if amplified in the brain of a scrod —

Whereas one cur might reasonably insist
    That it was science that got us into this,
Some other hound might justifiably propound
    That, *au contraire*, it was human stupidity;

But cannot all dogs agree
    That while human stupidity
Won't get us out of
    Anything at all

Science just might?

No?

Oh.

Hooter-snood on its radiator
    Honeywagon 2020 CE
Labors up the hill

Towards the '21 handoff,
    Plewds of sudoresis
Crown the exertion

Appurtenant to its burden
    Of malice, ill will, disease
And lies. "Don't you notice

A powerful and obnoxious
    Odor of mendacity
In this room?

It smells like death."
    What answer might Brick make,
Tonight, to Big Daddy's query?

"We study history," one of its teachers
    Once said to me, "so as to discern
How *useless* it's all been."

How distinct from Herodotus,
    Who undertook his *Historiê* "…so that
Human achievement may be spared

The ravages of time…."
    O Time!
Lord of the Boneyard!

Grant us the perspective
    Of Honeywagon 450 BCE
As the trash was cleared

From its swollen eyes
By the ragpickers of Oxyrhynchus!

No. 28   *1/5/2021*

    Sooner than later, Master Citizen-Baiter,
        Carbon-fiber snake-gaiters
    Become *couture de rigueur*
        Because, as in any election year,

    Perfervid bootlickers
        Spontaneously metempsychose
    Into the shin-fanging vipers
        They were when you hired them.

    It Is The Way.

    So, tog up: snake-gaiters for bloviators
        Plus chrome aviators
    To deflect incoming Walter Paters
        Whilst your flailing wrists disPence spinnerets

    Of favors, medals, pardons — what, no coinage?
        Like suction darts
    At the insatiable looking-glass
        Of your personal glaucoma. Give up

    The Bambi, for giving fawns a bad name,
        The Liberty Banana for Hypocrisy,
    A *summa cum laude* for Daily MacInanities,
        And be sure to be pollutedwaterjetting that special epitaph

    Onto the PlayDoh™ footstone
        Of Democracy:
    Boned by Greatness.

    Yonder thunders the Pale Rider
        Galloping to pin
    Her sundown spiculation
        Onto the steatopygous

Southbound boot
   Of the northbound
Loser's golf cart, while
   Threading her barbed lance

Through mendacious declamations
   Like shish-kabobical
Peccancies come due:
   "This seems to suggest

— Since the same tricks
   Which had failed Aristagoras,
One-on-one with Cleomenes,
   Had won round 30,000 Athenians —

That a crowd
   Is more easily fooled
Than a single man."
   Thus Herodotus

Outed the secret
   Of manipulating the Oikoumene
The "inhabited world"
   Some two thousand

Four hundred
   Fifty-two
Years before
   TV.

And hey, don't forget
   A statuette, or two, each,
For maquillage, haberdashery
   And inchoate prolixity,

Plus one inch of rotted codpiece
   On a dildonic plinth
For The Parking of The Collective Brain
   On the Bridge of Reality

Even as the brine rises to meet
    The dampening car-deck
Of every last bridge in Oikoumene.
    Last last but not least least

A Fiberboard Rhinhorn
    Aka The Buboed Truncheon
For most purpuric
    Chilblains per hectare per Pinocchio

(A metric of acceleration)

Withal portending perpetual winter
    Following the impact
Of the Meteor of Pseudoepistemics
    Implewding the Sea of Hebephrenics

Its lofting detritus
    Tuning out the sun,
Pending but hardly forfending
    The unslakable chromosphere of

El
    Señor
Red
    Giant

As it consumes the last
    Bit of frenetic fun,
And bequeaths
    The Music of Eschatology,

Squeals of space junk
    Crisping to cinders
As it circumrotates
    A phantom voxel

At the edge
    Of the only parsec
That this dumb movie
    Will ever colonize.

No. 29   *1/28/2021*

> As I was backfilling the lacuna
>   In my autodactython
> Baby Huey, the fuck,
>   Announced he was gone.
>
> It could have been a dummy
>   It could have been a drill
> It could be that democracy
>   Is over the hill
>
> It could be that some plutocrat
>   Took over the state
> And it could be that the media
>   Arrived early but it's too late
>
> It could be an earthquake
>   It could be a drill
> It could merely be that History
>   Has a little hole to fill.
>
> You might be kibble
>   On your master's bib
> You might even take the credit
>   That Eve came from your rib
>
> You might claim to be autochthonic
>   But only thieves have a lock on it
> Altogether this might be a high colonic
>   Though it's likely just a bitter pill
>
> That History, even multiphonic,
>   Just has a little hole to fill.
>
> So while the storm rages
>   And blows away all your pages
> And the wall, too,
>   Of your room,

It might be a tsunami
    Or a stone post on a hill
Nonetheless, while you're
    Wolfing my pastrami

History has a little hole to fill.

Yeah, it might be a jagged little pill —
    It might be two pills and a bolus —
Or maybe it's the just the internet
    Feeding on the *polis*

But all the usual suspects
    Plus a new wrinkle or two
Will succumb to the Manichean
    Stones of the mill

Cause History has no time
    For dialectics
History's
    Got a little hole to fill.

Looks, tastes, smells, sounds, parses,
    Cringes, yawns, stretches, swallows
Like Blunderthon, but hey,
    Time marches on

And History has a little hole to fill…

As I was backfilling
    A lacuna in my autodactython
Old Fill-In-The-Blank
    Announced he/she/it was gone

Don't be aw-shucksly sly shy
    Don't mewl like a shill
It ain't even he/she/its fault
    That History

Had a little hole to fill.

It coulda been a boyfriend
   It coulda been a girl
It coulda been a teacup
   On the giant Tilt-a-Whirl

Try not to puke

The marinade
   Is a cavalcade
Of flavors
   Yang and yin

If you want the din
   To take you serious
About lemonade or collagen
   You got to wear a suit

The exception
   Being Washington
Where 'serious'
   Is kinda moot

'Oumuamua, now
   Didn't come to stay
Took one look, castled the rook
   And made a getaway

After all,
   Any civilization
Whose mortification
   Is visible from space

Should be given
   All the room it needs
To evaporate
   Without a trace.

"Breathe deep the spring air,"
   A friend wrote to Clarice Lispector
In 1947, two months after
   The undersigned was born,

"Think as little as possible,
   And analyze even less."

Fat chance:

Whereas everybody else
   Ends with the apostrophe,
'Oumuamua
   Begins with it.

Gettum up Scout.

No. 31   2/2/2021

Here's how it goes
    It starts with a cough
Next thing you know
    The wheels are coming off

Then you're strapped in a lorry
    Not feeling too brainy
Especially when you realize
    You're feeling sorry for Liz Cheney

Bing! some dude in a mumu
    Is dealing you pills
And somebody's texting
    Your phone about bills

'Aspiration' takes on
    A whole new *Weltanschauung*
Since you went for that GED
    And say, that's a nice belt you got on

And while some post-doc emails
    About your *cuerpo* and science
A loudhailer on the wall
    Won't shut up till you grok self-reliance

And those perforations in the ceiling
    Each one's a wormhole
To a personal eternity, where the peeing is easy
    And the internet is free

Little pinch… We don't do
    Faxes anymore, but,
Before your feet hit the door
    Would you mind rating our service?

—What? Your name's not Purvis?
    Oh but — he must have been
The occupant previous
    This job makes me so nervous

Ever since they dialed the conveyor
    Way past ten
It's hard to keep track
    Who what died where, and when

In the front door, right out the back
    You should see how those boxes
In the parking lot are stacked
    But, all too true, I forget who I'm talking to

No matter, Pilgrim,
    Relax
Here's your last shot
    Now count backwards from ten…

Welcome to Texas.

No. 32

2/25/2021

Well I went to the doctor
   To get his point of view
What seems to be the matter, son
    Yo Doc, I got the pixilatin' blues.

I feel like we're bound to lose
   I'm walking on screws
I'm way into the booze
   'Cause I'm watching too much news

I scan it in the morning
   I scan it at night
I scan it in the bathtub
   My wig's in such a fright

Every day I squander a portion
   Of my energy fortune
On squalid luridities —
   Even though it's all already in Thucydides!

I'm afeared of sealing aforetime my
   troglomorphosis. I — Whoa!
The doc stopped me,
   Gripping his beard

By the Grateful Dead's roses,
   What prognosis is that?
Why, it's living in a hole
   Or descending into one

A brand new disease
   Bequeathed us by century twenty-one
By zero-sum games
   Like politics or chewing gum

By scrolling the feeds
   From sun to sun —
Or by owning more than one gun?
   Just to — he waggled his fingers — add to the fun?

Bingo, Doc, I see
   You're a quick study
So now maybe you descry
   Why my complexion's gone ruddy.

So the prescription's opium —
   Right? I prompted with hope
Does not Western Medicine
   Always go for the dope?

Hmmm, the Doc pinched his chin
   But he didn't open his pad
My tradition can't help you, son
   He pronounced, as if all sad

We're down to the scrip of fate:
   I'm afraid, in the cradle, you see,
You were dealt a pair
   His hand arced through the air

A pair of twos, moreover.
   May I make a suggestion?
Sure Doc, anything, let's have it.
   And the Doc patted his own tummy,

A playground of considerable girth,
   Go ahead, he said, play some gin rummy
Eat, drink and get chummy
   Don't worry: engorge till you burst!

Really, said I, that seems like
   Advice contrary to the notion of longevity
Or, I added thirstily,
   Are you just trying to be nice?

Not at all, the doc replied.
   I'm gonna ease you out gently
Feet first, I won't lie, but smooth
   With a proper salute from the sentry

So go ahead. Get fat.
   Cultivate a buzz. Nothing eschew!
Get down! Play it hot, 'cause if you do,
   Take it from me, cuz,

Something else might kill you
   Before the news does.

No. 33   *2/25/21*

    I think of the spirit of Lawrence

        in his djellaba

    rising over San Francisco,

        arms outstretched

    with voiceover

        "All this was bohemia..."

    Followed by thunder

No. 34

Hey, man, when's that surgery?
   11:45, next Thursday
Oh, so, not to worry
   There's plenty of time

Plenty of time
   To pay the bills
Plenty of time
   To make out that will

Plenty of time
   To jog over the hill
Take a shower and eat that
   Tower of pills

Plenty of time…

Plenty of time
   To excoriate the President
Plenty of time
   To note that my one and only

Is heaven-sent
   Plenty of time
To pay the rent
   Plenty of time

To bang out that dent
   To account for every cent
Oh, yeah,
   There's plenty of time.

Plenty of time

To pace to and fro
   Plenty of time
To get that duck in a row

Plenty of time
    To butcher a cow
Plenty of time
    To spile a plank on that scow

Plenty of time
    To mow the lawn
Plenty of time
    To un-pawn the clavinet

There might not be time to spawn
    But those days are over and gone
Which leaves
    Plenty of time...

When did you schedule that surgery?
    11:45 next Thursday
Oh, cool, that gives us time
    To have a drink, maybe even

Puke in the sink, like the old days,
    Before you gotta Zoom with your shrink
Did I tell you the reefer's on the blink?
    But you still got time to think

That clown
    In the gown
Is gonna cut
    On you

While he's listening
    To Django
And the
    Rubinoos

He'll be done
    Before you know he's through
There's a copay
    Even if the biopsy is blue

After which
    You'll have plenty of time
To reflect
    On single-payer modality

And to discuss Israel
    Over a cup of tea
To watch the tide
    Come in and go out

To watch that albatross
    Glide over the sea

Plenty of time
    Oh yeah

Plenty of time…

No. 35

4/7/2021

  …and while you're out back
   Taking a piss
    Reflect on this

  You gotta have a website
  To prove you exist.

  Not the lesson you sought
   At the breast of History
    Along with:

  Legion are the begettors of misery
   Who never get caught

  And every equilibrium is fraught
   By turbulence of thought —

  Excepting the ones you pay for
   Till your purse sighs with emptiness
    Like a zeppelin lanced

  By the certainty of chance
   And bam! you're back
    To zeroes bestirred by ones

  Bones animated by flesh
   Like the mandibles of an ant
    In some parallel dimension

  Reaching into this one
   To snug the cord on your *kabuto*
    For a fight it's got no skin in

  Not unlike the dreidel of your disbelief
   Tracing coils in the colloidial suspension
    Till the friction of spin is spun

Job done, under the guise of Fate
    Done regardless, even in darkness,
        Mind numb, so what, why wait?

De rigueur pins and needles
    In the extremities, the tingle
        Of an awareness

That will never arrive.
    And yet you survive

To start awake stark naked
    On the compacted sand of the pugil pit
        Confronted by a Cheetocephalic

Dung beetle, badly drawn,
    Wanton to roll another one.
        Just before its foetid breath

Fogs your visor, the features
    Of an intimate, long claimed by death,
        Assemble on the overhead score-keeping

Tesseract, its chiaroscuro lips
    Discreetly let slip that, perhaps,
        You've forgotten something?

Daffodils, maybe?
    A pocket knife?
        Spring?

No. 36

It seems to me
  Said Titus Quinctius
    Opening his hands to the fire

That Death releases us
  Into this life
    Then reclaims us

Willy-nilly, according to the rules
  Of a great game
    We'll never understand.

A knot popped,
  Lofting a spark
    Into the darkness.

A few of us, indeed,
  Marcus Acilius replied,
    As he drew a scrap of stone

Along the length of his blade,
  Loom as if unleashed
    Onto life itself,

While the majority might claim,
  and not without reason,
    That it's life itself

That's unleashed
  On the wretched
    Rest of us.

Short or tall, fat or thin
  Knees unstrung by disease
    Or obdurate cataclysm,

Shave your head
  And get on with it —
    Or History will shave it for you!

Yes, muttered Quinctius,
  His breath visible in the cold,
    History the beancounter,

The gourmet,
  The unrelenting
    Custodian of death.

Selecting a length
  Of bright blade at random
    Acilius shaved an inch of hair

Off the back of his wrist,
  Puffing the short ends
    Towards the fire.

With a grunt of approval,
  He stood out of his cloak
    And sheathed the sword,

Greaves gleaming,
  Even by firelight
    His scars manifest.

"Let's go."

No. 37

I knew an anthropoid Baby Huey
   And he'd dance for you
      In Oxford brogans

Rayon hair, prolapsed cravat
   And baggy pants
      The old soft shoe

He'd limbo so low
   Limbo so low
      Purse his lips

And extrude a big lie,
   Polishing thereby, and
      Not-so-damn-shy,

The communal clown…

Oh, Baby Huey
   Say hey, Baby Huey
      Wash your hands, Baby Huey

Then dance...

I met him first to last
   On a television screen,
      I was down and out

He braced me with squinty eyes
   Of calculated rage
      and he began to spout

He talked of life
   As nobody ever lived it
      Talked of life

Then he'd clench his fist
   Click his heels
      And improvise,

More and yet more
> *Ex tempore ad nauseum*
>> Back and forth across

The pixelatin' proscenium
> As the sun went down
>> On majority rule…

He elicited scared laughs
> Maybe even ten or twelve million
>> Until he lost flat out

Flat out lost
> Face plant on the rostrum
>> For and by the count

Which suited many people
> World around
>> Right down to the ground…

Oh, Baby Huey
> Yo, Baby Huey
>> You lost, Baby Huey

Dance…

He danced for those
> In minstrel shows
>> And county fairs

Throughout the south

He spoke, near tears,
> Of the two or three years
>> When his blog and him

Traveled about

Then the blog up and died
> The blog up and died
>> After twenty years

He'll still grieve…

He fondly told how he'd dance
   Just give him a chance
      For tips and winks

But now most of his time
   He lolls on his links
      Cheating the back nine

Cause he confabulates a bit
   Still confabulates a bit
      As he marinates in his brine

He's waitin' for someone,
   To tell the truth anyone,
      Just anyone to ask him: Hey,

Aren't you Baby Huey?
   Yo, it's Baby Huey!
      Say hey, Baby Huey

Won't ya please dance…?

— w/ apologies to
Mr. Jerry Jeff Walker

No. 38 6/8/2021

> The proscenium entrance
>   To every cemetery
>   Should feature a clock
>
> Surmounted by the motto
>   Mark the time, hominid,
>   And, below,
>
> Do you know where your soul is?
>
> This *horologe* should be analog,
>   With comely fletched arrows
>   And Roman numerals
>
> Twelve XIIs because,
>   Well, *you* know, it's always
>   Midnight somewhere,
>
> So, no matter, and despite
>   Its locus, your soul
>   Will recognize the chime.
>
> The gates between the jambs
>   Should never be locked
>   Nor even closed
>
> And the light within
>   Ghostly and thin
>   Sourceless and dim
>
> Just bright enough to limn
>   Street names and epitaphs —
>   O epitaphs!
>
> All of which sum to
>   Once I was as you are
>   And you shall be as I am.

The mouth of Upside Down
  Horseshoe Road
    A cul-de-sac

Is bridged by
  Equable Boulevard
    Which tees into

Epistemectomy Lane
  At one end
    And Positivist's Leap

At the other.
  The Boulevard of Fatuity
    Meanders to the Promenade of Vacuity

All of them one-way
  Excepting
    The Bascule of Promiscuity

Which is co-dimensional
  With the Möbius Party Strip.
    Though densely planted

Worry not: like the length
  Of its leafy neighbor
    Vicolo Tempus Tacendi

There is quiet everywhere,

Tranquil and still
  The contrapositive of shrill —
    If you can't hear it, it's not loud,

I.e.,
  The hole
    Not the drill.

Below the Leap
   The Plain of Jars
     Extends as far

As the eye can see.
   And really,
     Churlish tourist,

Feel free
   To bomb the shit
     Out of it

Before you
   Make yourself
     At home.

No. 39

7/12/2021

So now the plague
  Hath run its course
    Though perhaps its allele

Doth abide, perfectly still,
  Like a coney in the gorse
    Or, like coyote,

Stalks the rhinoscape
  Alert to weakness—*or*
    Maybe it's ravaging the 3rd World?—*or*

Maybe it never existed in the first place!
  Simón grins the calavera
    ¡Quizás los tres!

He/She/It clatters a splintered toothpick
  Along the row of broken teeth
    Like the ribs of a *güiro*,

The mocking stridulation
  Of a jaded
    Ur-cicada.

Have you never
  Thought about
    The trip to Texas

When your time comes?
  Put another way,
    Rather than spend all day

Complaining about life
  Why not spend all night
    Complaining about death?

(Uh... Is that the contrapositive?)

On the third hand,
   I interrupted,

Donald Fucking Rumsfeld
Donald Fucking Rumsfled

Edith M. Bell
Edith M. Bell

Scheise, says the skull,
  Removing the tapered sliver
    And inspecting its tip,

That's a little too
  West Coast
    Literary for me.

Not to worry, I pointed out;
  Cut to the chase, it scans
    But it doesn't add up.

In other words, Mr. In-Between,
  To rephrase the question,
    What's with all these Donalds

Mucking up History, of late?
  Jeeze, dissembled the unhinged mandible,
    Like Stendhal said —.

Dang and whoa, uncorked I,
  Whaddya mean,
    Like Stendhal said?

A mention of politics
  (The venerable *Totenkopf*
    Paraphrased sententiously)

In polite conversation
  Is like a pistol shot
    At a concert.

Oh.
  [Pause.]
    Were we being polite?

— A-a-and hey, while we're at it,
  May I point out, I pointed out,
    That to answer a question

With another question
  Is a rhetorical no-no?
    The oxidized pincers of your

Saline vituperation
  Heap me with
    Tomographic introspection,

 The sagittal crest,
  Though of bone,
    Glowered as the jaw groused. But,

Vis à vis
  The branding of History
    I'll have to get back to you;

Adding, with the inflection
  Of disdain, You do
    Have time to wait?

Oh sure, replied I,
  I got time.
    I'll just stand here

Maybe lean against this wall
  Have a smoke
    Order a drink

As the flinders
Scatter to windward.

No. 40

The bard sat
  With her back to a
    Lichened stone wall

Dry-set and coutoured
  With ivy. And ticks?
    Arachne forfend

And politics damn all,
  Plink a plink, plink plink,
    Plink a plink.

Her six-string was slim
  Its top, close-grained,
    Quite blonde, and its bout a sveldt

Twelve inches. A sliver of tibia
  Formed its nut; its fretboard and
    Bridge were of ebony; its

Tailpiece a caiman snout.
  And those unbending fat
    Flat-wound strings?

A sonorous, mellifluous
  Plink a plink, plink plink,
    plink a plink.

So enamoured was she
  With scales in all keys
    That she failed to discern

The testudo's approach,
  Clank a thud, thud thud,
    Clank a thud,

Till fenced by boots
   Her fate become moot —
     Though at first

Her plonk merely
   Did the lads broach.
     Soon enough, perforce,

The column reformed
   Three abreast, ineluctable
     Its march. The bard's *zahako*

Shuttled perpendicular
   To the vector of advance,
     Warp to the woof of war,

'Til, sucked dry,
   'Twas punted aside, and
     The bard's head, surprised,

Dangling by its hair
   From the belt of the hoplite
     In the middle, watched it go.

He had the guitar too
   And while his mate
     Held his *sarissa*

He assayed without peer
   The string that remained,
     Plink a thud

Thud thud
   Plink a thud —
     Until,

Perforce,
   The terrain
     Became mud,

And, Lugh
  Prevailing,
    Inflected by gorse.

Finally, by and by,
  The guitar of a piece,
    Kindled the squadron's campfire,

Its heat waxed brief
  Til the purfling expired,
    And the cold closed down for real.

Now a moral,
  I'm certain,
    Is required.

And I wish
  I had one,
    Even bland.

If you've a talent
  I'd guess
    Try your mortal best

To leaven evil
  With the touch
    Of your hand — yah?

Leaven evil
  With the touch
    Of your hand.

Maybe so,
  Plink a plink,
    Maybe so.

Plink plink
  Plink a plink
    Maybe so.

No. 41

Every time I peel garlic
   I think of Arthur Okamura
      Who hated to peel garlic.

Kitty and I
   Would stand aside
      As Arthur attacked a clove

Disporting, dare I say,
   The ineluctable scowl
      Of an annoyed warrior,

A demeanor entirely belied
   By the serenity of his art.
      Once, sous-chefery dispensed,

Arthur took me to the studio
   To show me his latest painting,
      Big as a door,

Of rain pelting down
   Through the segmented shafts
      Of a dark bamboo grove.

He pointed: How'd I do that?
   I shook my head.
      Come on, Jim,

You're a carpenter! By the hint
   Unbeguiled, I shrugged.
      Then Arthur showed me

His chalkbox.
   Of course!
      Each drop

Plummeted a neat line
   Angled from top
     To bottom

Of the frame: Snap!
   Et voilà —
     Rain!

I snip each end
   Of the clove
     Then crush it

With a cheap cleaver
   Purchased on Grant Avenue
     In Chinatown

At the dawn
   Of culinary expertise.
     Roll off the paper,

Dice the clove.
   And I think, too,
     Of the guy who owned

The Villa Hermosa
   At Haste, across Telegraph
     From Cody's Books,

Who always sat at a table
   Just inside the front door,
     With apron and knife,

Before him a proper
   Porcelain charger
     Heaped a foot high

With pale whole cloves,
   Gleaming, uncrushed,
     Perfectly peeled

Until, one day,
   He'd sold enough
      Delectable rellenos,

Tostadas and chicken molé
   To retire to Jalisco, where he owned
      Two more restaurants

And housing sufficient
   To domicile and employ
      All of his many

Children and grandchildren.
   And who — not I —
      Can forget

Jewel and Darl and Tull diving
   The river for a drowned chalkbox
      After a log-rolling current

Had swept the family wagon,
   Ma Bundrin's coffin, the mules,
      And all of Cash's tools

Off the surging bridge?
   In the same novel
      Can be found the line,

"How often have I lain beneath
   Rain on a strange roof
      Thinking of home?"

I didn't think
   To bring it up
      With Arthur that day

But, looking at the bamboo
   In his painting then
      One could hear

The steaking rain
   Bearing down
      On a tin roof

Before dawn, and how it meant
   No work today,
      Carpenter.

Insofar as I'm aware,
   That's about it
      For chalkbox lit.

Come to supper.

No. 42   11/27/2021

The interweb is not making it
  Woe is me
    Though I'm rooting

For Baby Huey
  The Duke of Louche
    As he courts his apocheetosis.

Meanwhile, no, the interweb
  Isn't making it.
    I fret and rock

Rock and fret
  Minutes pass like subluminal parsecs
    The dopamine pump lurks

At its charging station
  No taste like the first taste
    Can't remember the last taste

C.f. the definition of Fate
  Aka Facebait
    Study your reflection

Pixelated by ingathered data
  You, comrade, know
    What's coming next

The off-rhyme of Meta
  Way, way off.
    And here's a prediction:

In 2023, or thereabouts,
  About a year
    Before the presidential election,

Little Lord VoldeMark will cede
  Baby Huey's Facebait account
    Back to him/her/it

On the bet that,
  If he/she/it wins
    For him/her/its

Department of Justice,
  In louchestep
    With the Louche Gnosis,

And the game of Monopoly™®©,
  It will be hands off
    Facebait: after all,

What's the loss of a few
  Developing minds
    As opposed to

Owning Kauai?
  As go Transactional Endgames,
    A Square Deal

As most any
  Dispassionate observer
    Will have to admit.

Nothing personal,
  Comrade.
    After all,

It's not about you
  It's about your Data —
    Unless, of course,

You don't shop enough.
  Like I said,
    The interweb

Isn't making it,
  Not for me,
    Not for you

Either. No,
  It's making It
    For Itself.

One day soon
  VoldeMark will check
  His cheetosiatin' rug

In his own
  Pixelatin' mirror
    And see for himself

The kerb to which,
  Soon than later,
    Fate will be kicking his pale ass,

And just in time, too,
  Just before
    The last thing

That passes through
  Humanity's mind
    As humanity hits

The windshield of history
  Will be humanity's phone.
    Thumbs up!

No. 43 — 12/23/2021

More gravid with diktat
  Than a David
    Lean long shot

Nobody ever asks me
  About my Process
    Is it kegels and lox

(No?) or one-putts
  And eagles
    (Yes?)

Sitting by a roaring fire
  Reading *Voices From Chernobyl*
    Does it get any better?

One thing seems certain:
  The stupid arm themselves
    Kill with abandon

Then, just like that,
  Killers and killed
    Fade into History.

If you've got a gun
  And time on your hands
    What's not to like?

No. 44

1/13/2022

    My cohort are croaking
      I don't know what to do
        Long gone the days of storking

(I must run to the loo)

On Next Door
  An entity posts
    "Is it only me

That's just found out
  That omicron
    Is a letter

In the Greek alphabet?"
   Well, amigo, at my house,
     Right next door,

It is just you.
  Not only that,
    But omicron is merely

The 15th letter
  In the Greek alphabet.
    My advice to you?

Stay tuned, Neighbor!

No. 45

Bhangmeter

Look, mon
  If it has to be done
    I'd rather contract

My Covid-19
  From mouth-to-mouth resuscitation
    Of a pulseless surfer

Boy or girl
  Washed up
    On Rodeo Beach

On a big day
  As opposed to,
    Say,

An air kiss
  Deployed by a
    Republican doyenne

Boy or girl,
  Flown in
    For the memorial

Of a guy, boy or girl,
  We both knew forever
    Whose phantom connects us

Via the withered
  Dendrites
    Of nostalgia.

A mouthful
  Broken up
    For your delectation.

That's just the way I feel.

Okay?
  In fact,
    That's exactly

The way
  I feel.
    I –.

Sure,
  Mr. Nisbet.
    Sure?

Of course!
  Oh.
    Better now?

Uh…
  No remorse?
    I…

Got it all sorted?
  Less tension?
    Oh, tension. Yeah.

Yeah. Well good,
  Mr. Nisbet. Drink
    Some of this.

Oh,
  Yeah
    Yeah.

Now
  Put your hand here.
    Oh,

Yeah yeah.
  Now for some pills…
    Oh,

Yeah, yeah.
  Now look.
    Yeah?

There.
  Yeah.

It's

The 49ers
  Versus the Bills,
    Mr. Nisbet.

Oh
  Yeah
    Yeah…

With all due respect
To Mr. Charles Bukoski

No. 46 1/26/2022

    Baby Huey
       Aka The Duke of Louche
         Aka *Boca del Terremoto*

    Aka *Deditos de Pollo*
       Aka *Completamente Calva*
         Egualmente Pelado

   – Earthquake Mouth
      With Little Chickenfingers,
      Bald and Skint To Boot–

    Not to mention
      Les Plus Grand
        Pendejo –

    The Biggest
      Pubic Hair – with
        Cranium of Porridge

    Short on Storage
      Putin's Bitch
        With a brain

    Like a Bibi
      In a shoebox,
        Revanchist with a Lost Cause

    Reactionary solely via
      Transactional Expedience,
        An unrepentant pustule

    Migrating to the nether parts
      Of History
        Where he will

Never be alone:
   Would it do any good
     To remind him

That there's always
  A Bigger Motherfucker,
    One more suppurant,

Viscid, flushed, fungal,
  Glutinous, mucal and
    Pale, more

Intolerant of the weak,
  The meek,
    The disadvantaged,

The irradiated, the flooded,
  The choked? Bigger
    Than he and all the other

Small-time
  Motherfuckers
    Clustered

In the foetid
  Fundament
    Of History?

Mellow yellow furrow!

He, for whom
  The echo-
    Chamber

Was invented,
  May yet get
    Clobbered

By the reverberations
   Of his own
      Bullshit.

After all, as
   Deep Science
      Tells us,

Shock waves pass
   Right through
      Bullshit,

Scything its DNA
   Nucleotide
      By nucleotide,

Their power
   Contrapositive
      And undiminished

I can't wait.

No. 47

2/10/2022

My zeitgeist
  Lies bleached
    On the mountain

The mule
  Of ambition
    Heads for the sea

The beads
  Of the abacus
    Are countin'

The comebacks
  Are dwindling
    For me.

That mortician
  Whittles
    His trocar

The Mandelbröt
  Diverges
    To naught

The vicar
  Kisses
    Her ankh

On TV, a tuxedoed monkey
  Stanches the
    President's wounds

With crushed insects
  From MOMA's
    Septic tank.

Despite which vision…

Far afield we wander
   In search of the brazing
     Bromides of mendacity

In service of the
   Pseudo-anneal
     Of the communal roar

Every man *sieg heils*
   En masse
     Every man

Dies alone.
   No need
     To explain this

To the solitary widow
   [Sanskrit for emptiness]
     Ancient knowledge

Writ large
   So large
     Few

Can read it.

"Both ancient and modern writers have
used the Battle of Thermopylae as
an example of the power of an army
defending its native soil."— Wikipedia

Well do I remember,
  In the runup to the
    Invasion of Iraq (2003, CE),

An American general
  Bidding his radio
    Audience to imagine

That it lives in Tulsa
  Only to find itself
    Completely surrounded

By an enormous hostile force
  Whose perimeter precisely defines
    The borders of Oklahoma.

"You'd surrender
  Wouldn't ya? Huh?
    Lay down your arms

And give up. Right?
  Of course you would."
    Flash forward to

February 24, 2022, CE:
  "Ahoy,
    Snake Island,

This is Russian ship.
  You are completely
    Surrounded.

Lay down your weapons
  Or die." After a moment
    Of radio silence:

"Russian ship, go fuck yourself." And
  Kablooey. The entire garrison,

Thirteen Ukranians
  Defending zero point
    Seven square kilometers,

Take their place in History,
  And a nation called Russia
    Resumes its effacement

From those same pages,
  Destined to be no less forgotten
    Than Xerxes Uno and his much vaster

Achaemenid Empire.
  While the American general
    Was wrong about Baghdad,

Might not he just as well
  Have been whispering
    Into Vlad The Impaler's

Tinnitic earbone, deep in the echoing
  Vlaborhinth, as
    Bloviating on NPR?

One wonders if that guy
  Is available today, still alive
    To fly his desk

Straight into the mirror of
  Thirteen pairs of Snake-eyes
    As they stare back from the green

Felt table of Fate
   Their twinned dots
      Forever reflected

In the row of thirteen beribboned
   Medallions, their tin enfiladed
      Across boyo's breast

Twelve of them awarded
   For sage advice
      And one for cowardice.

No. 49   *2/28/2022*

O-ho can you breed
By the fawn set alight?
What so loudly you brailed
At the fluid's last draining,
   Not to mention
Fractured mentors long spurned
For their antifascist leanings.

And the lucre's green blare
Gave truth to the blight
Of Citizens United
And the drift to the right.

O bray lest ye seethe
Though Kapital's Katheter peeve
And the mandible of minimum wage
Strikes fear into the unsaved
And though the Rand of the counterfactual
Saves naught but the few
We sang to Bruce through the night
Though the lyrics no one knew.

Let's start this again
   We're all conceived in sin
Though a silver spoon in the mouth
   Beats being born black in the south.
And —
   Confidential to the Pillsbury Doughboy —
Dude,
   The more you explain to us about everything
The less we think you know about anything
   And your escapades into ersatz oratory
Come across as sleigh-bell minatory
   Just sayin'. O

Pray you don't forget your obeisant braille
   Even as you're being waterboarded
Pray your dreams don't set sail
   While you're being overlorded

Them geese overhead
   Are leaving without you
And they just might survive
   Your plastic without you,

Too.

And the rockets' Red glare?
   Through the night stay tuned
      'Cause Vlad the Impaler

Is watching from the moon.

No. 50   *3/14/2022*

    The peat stopper of foetid Infamy
      Corks the porcelain flagon
        Of fragrant Progress:

Now, Elon! Now, Jeffery! Now,
  Raymond and Freeman!
    Was it Arthur C. Clarke,

Asked if the human race
  Might one day
    Colonize the stars,

Who dourly declared,
  "The civilization capable
    Of interstellar travel

Will blow itself up first."
  What a killjoy!
    On the other hand,

Who, these days —
  Which is
    Most days —

Thinks
  It's even close?
    Put another way:

The Big Kablooey
  Looms to arrive
    Long before interstellar

Aspirations
  Will find the moxie
    To soil their short pants.

But dash away, fellas!
  Don't be discouraged!
    Dash away all!

While the balance of us,
  99.999% of us, needn't further roil
    Our meager reservoirs

Of news-besotted glucose,
  For — behold,
    Hail, yo,

Bear witness to
  Yon tardigrades
    Standing back and by

Between the furrows
  Of every middle brow
    On the planet,

Patent to inherit
  The radiogenic flinders.
    The etymology

Is "slow-stepper",
  But, sooner or later,
    After they've o'ertaken us,

They'll cool one
  Till the corona of a dying sun
    Envelopes the blue marble entire

And thusly,
  You see,
    A star comes to thee.

No. 51

    All I did
      Was take a break
        But somehow I gave Vlad

    The time to create
      His own planetesimal
        From which to harass

    All the rest of us.
      Oh, the mundane was in place —
        It was everywhere: the pot of tea,

    The cheap cologne,
      The pseudo-Chechens
        Blowing up apartment buildings

    Where they don't even speak the language,
      The lawyer
        Starved on a bench

    The smelly heresiarch soothed
      By the petty gaoling
        Of a couple of naive girls

      The affronted teenaged buildungsgroman,
        That yet manages to take account
          Of the need,

    Of the corruption assumed native
      To all the pale brothers
        The chalky, pre-besuited brothers

    All of a certain age
      Of a certain persuasion
        — the pawl engages here,

The ratchet arrests it there,
   The wheel advances thus — it does not,
     You see,

Retreat. Ever.
   So the one-sixteenth of of an inch of steel
     Skimmed off the skins of every tank

Facing west between the Urals and Moscow
   Now hulling yon yacht's wondrous displacement, featuring
     A giant brown basilisk behind the saloon bar

 Whose jello shots are so tasty
   Because they aren't made of jello
     Beneath the faceted ball:

Aspirational — no?

No. 52   *6/11/2022*

    For Charlie Palau

Calico
  That's the fabric
    Little flowers

In an unbleached field
  And there're monarchs
    You remember monarchs

Don't you, amigo?
  Flocking the purlieus
    Of ye eucalyptical cudgel —

Or madrone —, this being
  California
    He's running

Further into. Of yore it
  Might well have been a limber cane
    Taper, ten foot or more,

With a friction cork and # 6 snelled hook
  Perfect for perch or bream.
    But this is not him.

Nor is this our petite
  Entonnant voyageur
    Reduced at last

To weeping
  Among the shards
    In the cockpit of possibilities.

No. This is the kid
  With the calico satchel,
    All of William Blake in there,

Toothbrush, notebook and pen,
  And this is his
    Last selfie.

The Dialogues
  Of Eternity
    Cook down

To phonemes of black.
  Trust me,
    I just got back.

Of weeping there is a surfeit
  Of laughter a modest cairn
    But all Gravity is thinking about

Is heading for the barn
  Where massless oblivions
    Do spiral their monopoles.

Final hemorrhages of images
  Not to worry, just watch 'em go by.
    They got no handles.

I'm ready to leave
  But my boot keeps
    Missing the stirrup

When I pause
  To breathe
    I hear the cricket's chirrup.

PHOTO: © DAVID LIITTSCHWAGER

Novelist and poet Jim Nisbet was a seminal figure in the West Coast Noir Renaissance. His early novels were published with the original Black Lizard Press, gaining Nisbet an international reputation as a fiercely unique voice whose work defied easy classification. He went on to publish more than a dozen novels, widely translated, with editions in France (by Rivages, under legendary editor François Guérif), Germany, Italy, and more. The author of seven collections of poetry, including a translation of Baudelaire, he published essays and other work in an eclectic mix of international journals and magazines. Nisbet grew up in North Carolina. After graduating from UNC Chapel Hill, he headed out to San Francisco, where he lived for many years, immersed simultaneously in the intellectual life — in his career as a working writer — and his daily work as a cabinetmaker and tradesman. *The Plague Ditties* was his last book, written during the worldwide pandemic, and completed shortly before his death in 2022.

www.ingramcontent.com/pod-product-compliance
Lightning Source LLC
Chambersburg PA
CBHW030157100526
44592CB00009B/326